Designed by Flowerpot Press in Franklin, TN.
www.FlowerpotPress.com
Designer: Jonas Fearon Bell
Editor: Johannah Gilman Paiva
PAB-0808-0120
ISBN: 978-1-4867-0556-6
Made in China/Fabriqué en Chine

Why Do Rainbows Have So Many Colors?

Written by
Jennifer Shand

Illustrated by
Daniele Fabbri

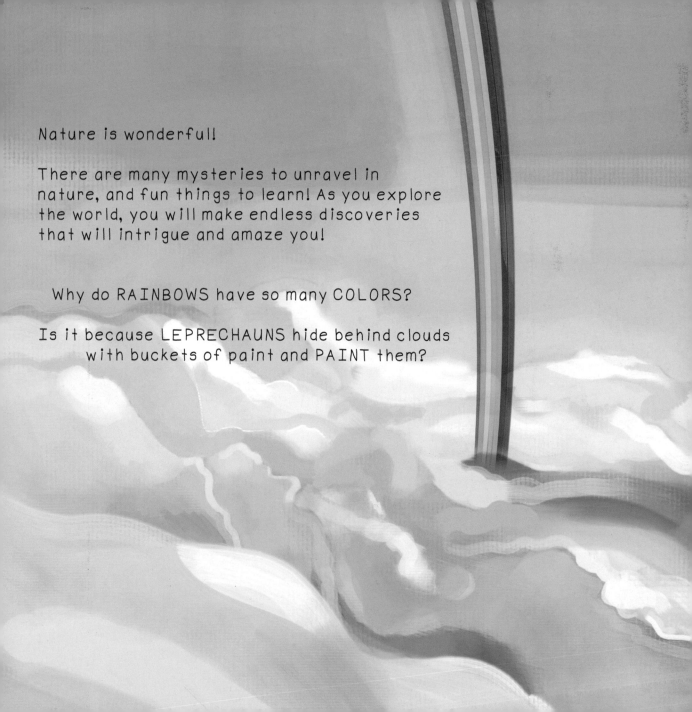

Nature is wonderful!

There are many mysteries to unravel in nature, and fun things to learn! As you explore the world, you will make endless discoveries that will intrigue and amaze you!

Why do RAINBOWS have so many COLORS?

Is it because LEPRECHAUNS hide behind clouds with buckets of paint and PAINT them?

No, that's silly!

Rainbows have many colors because
they are made from reflected sunlight,
and sunlight is actually made of lots of
different colors! Sunlight normally shines
as white light, but when that white light
hits the rain, the rain causes it to separate
into red, orange, yellow, green, blue, indigo,
and violet.

This makes a beautiful rainbow!

Why do some TREES lose all their LEAVES?

Is it because they love to DANCE
and accidentally SHAKE off all their leaves?

No, that's silly!

Trees lose their leaves because it helps them survive cold or dry weather! Shedding leaves helps the trees to conserve (or use less) water, food, and energy to make it through the parts of the year that are colder or drier. Only some trees do this, and they are called "deciduous trees." Before the leaves shed, though, they change from green to all sorts of beautiful colors!

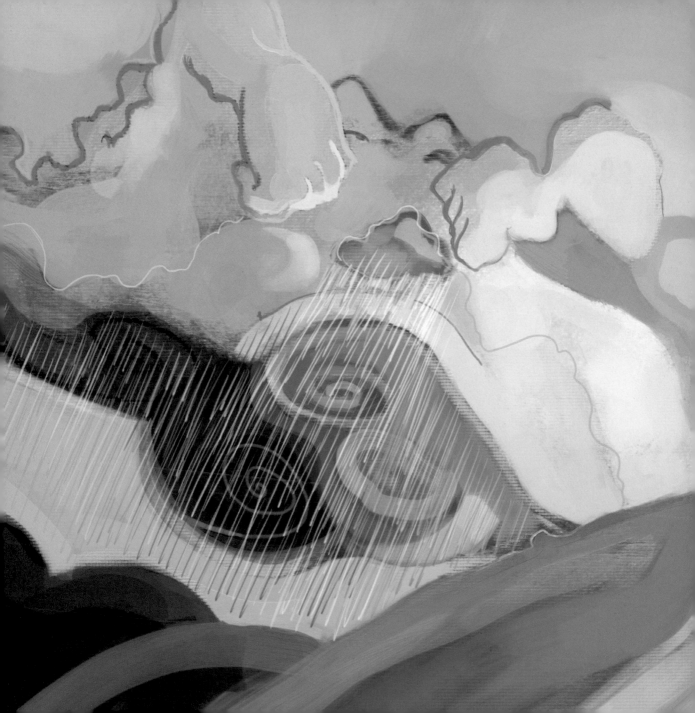

Why do some CLOUDS have rain FALLING out of them?

Is it because they are CRYING
and the rain is their TEARS?

Some clouds have rain falling because they get too full of water! The hot sun causes water from the ground to evaporate and rise up into the sky. Then, these tiny droplets cool and form clouds. As the clouds grow, and gather more and more water, the water droplets combine and get bigger, and once they get too heavy, the water falls out as rain!

Why do VOLCANOES stay quiet for so long and then suddenly ERUPT?

Is it because they didn't GET THEIR WAY
and are throwing a TANTRUM?

No, that's silly!

A volcano erupts when pressure from gases inside it build up so much that the volcano cannot contain them.

Volcanoes have melted rock, or "magma" inside of them, and magma has gases inside of it. From these gases, bubbles start to form, and this builds extreme pressure. This pressure makes the magma rise higher and higher until finally it is forced out of the volcano and spews into the air!

Once the magma is outside of the volcano, it is known as "lava."

Why do FLOWERS smell so GOOD?

Is it because they SPRAY PERFUME all over themselves?

No, that's silly!

Flowers smell so good because they are trying to attract insects, birds, and other animals to them. Their pleasant smell comes from their nectar. Flowers need animals to transfer their pollen from flower to flower in order to have "pollination." Pollination leads to seeds, which will lead to more flowers! A flower smelling good is nature's way of making sure we will always have more flowers!

Nature is amazing!

There are so many wonderful things to discover! Try to spot a rainbow, find a flower to smell, or listen to the sound of fall leaves crunching beneath your feet.

It's great to go out into nature, explore, and have fun!